Kamau Brathwaite

elegguas

WESLEYAN UNIVERSITY PRESS

MIDDLETOWN, CONNECTICUT

D1292677

Published by
WESLEYAN UNIVERSITY PRESS
Middletown, CT 06459
www.wesleyan.edu/wespress
© 2010 by Kamau Brathwaite
Printed in the United States of America
5 4 3 2 1

The Driftless Series is funded by the
Beatrice Fox Auerbach Foundation Fund
at the Hartford Foundation for Public Giving.

The Letters to Zea Mexican in this book
originally appeared in *The Zea Mexican Diary*,
Wisconsin University Press, 1993.

Library of Congress Cataloging-in-Publication Data
Brathwaite, Kamau, 1930–
Elegguas / Kamau Brathwaite.
    p. cm. — (Wesleyan poetry)
ISBN 978-0-8195-6943-1 (cloth : alk. paper) I. Title.
PR9230.9.B68E44   2009
811'.54—dc22   2009035923

This project is supported in part by an award
from the National Endowment for the Arts.

NATIONAL
ENDOWMENT
FOR THE ARTS
A great nation
deserves great art.

for

Timothy Reiss
&
Janice Whittle da Barbade

elegguas

. . . a long way from nan guinnen . . .

one

two

tree

four

five

one

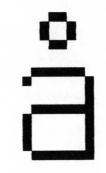

Letter to Zea Mexican

Sunday 14 Sept 1986

2 am

Dearest Mexican

Tomorrow afternoon I'll see yr face <
for the last time - see you for the lass
lass time I really cyaaan imagine th-
at yu know

From the very first I see you I know
. I certain . I sure. And I have alway
(s) been secure w/you Standing near
to you at Mother's funeral when I mi
ght have tumble into the grave - at
least that's how I feel - or when my hea
(d) was spinning in that bathroom
in the village of Bottisham nr Cam-<
bridge or in our little bedroom high
up in Irish Tn & I shouted out & yu
come running & hold me & tell me
not to worry that it wd pass Or when
it felt like fainting at Massachusetts
in all that snow on the way to GK >>
Hall (of all palaces - the first - but not
the last! - betrayal by a royal publish-
ers) or in that midday in the midd-
le of Delhi when it was so hot and <<

all that **pollution** - eternal dust it seem
from the desert of the city - & again yu
tell me I cd do it. You always say th-
at & I believe you because I *beleeve* in
you I **trust** in you & I know you cd
be trusted even too. What a wonder-
ful thing I realize now. I always kno
that nothing cd come between us I <<
kno for instance that if a gunman >>
was to come inside the house [it happen
later when you gone when i am alone: see ¶¶R]
we wd probably die together die for
each other w/each other I certainly
kno that I wd die for you if/when I
had to & you I'm even surer wd have
die for me as you almost once did as
it is . like when one day at Round <<
House the prop-up duncks tree by th
(e) backdoor steps start to fall on me
an before i cd blink or say Jackie Ro
binson my Mother was holding up
tha tree w/she body w/she feet wide
planting apart pun th hot red steps
of th house and i kno that that cudd-
(a) be yu an it make a whole world a
difference let me tell yu. . .

    Seems such a short time
we are together In fact feels like no
time at all Our 26 years already
here gone *'contracted to a span'* as
        my sister xplains
it but let's hope that it'll lengthen
back out to where we are now. Ev
-eryone has been wonderful
supportive etc [little did I know

4

that this wd not last wd not continue] tho
of course I continue to be like dumb
like dark/shut down & cannot be
console(d). How cd I ever be!

Each day I come to love you more
& more appreciate you more & more
So that Sarah cd write that even tho
she don't see so much of you
in London in recent years
[cf the Caribbean Artists Movement]
I always bring yr presence w/mwe

And as i tell you several times
during & after Massachusetts
& the Eagle there was
- cd be - no one else no matter what
yu or anybody else might think
or say

This was the golden time
finding as I say our own lifestyle
at/in IT-Penlyne-Bdos & the trips
abroad & Velma painting word
-pictures
- & how greedily i believe them & why not!
- of you & me at IT growin old like
once upon a time & doddery
but everlastinglovingly she smile to
-gether

George is here & is ecstatic about the
house [at Irish Tn - IT] & full of ideas
for improvement. Seems so strange
& such a pity that we nvr invited
him over even for a brief weekend/to

which I hear you say But doan mine
Georgel I always askin when he <<
comin & he always busy-busy-busy -
& George himself confirm this. Say
yu always invitin him but he always
too busy busy busy But now he's <<<
here, one wishes it cd have been the <
two of you together laughin gaffin <
loud & happily & tramping up & <<
down the place - an *now i think it like it*
really happen! - yu w/yr off-white jipp-
pa-jappa on, looking at where 'the <
road' wd be etc etc etc

Am sorry too we nvr phone Aunt El
eanor at least from time to time - kee
(p) more in touch w/them altho a-<<
gain I hear you laugh w/love Aunt <
Eleanor too confuse & of course th-
ere wd be time there wd be time ano-
ther time etc etc etc *But the phone was*
loud & clear when I get thru to New Am-
sterdam - God clearin the way to Uncle <
Time as it turn out to be & after shock <
& disbelief - he seem to take it cool - his
culture too polite to hurt me w/his pain - *re-*
lieve that - as he say - it was a good thing
itwas he pick up the phone because *if it*
was Eleanor he say *it surely wd have*
kill her - altho i kno they cd not think - im
agine - *that she dead an so is only me res-*
ponsible fe she & kill she - let she dead -
and I ask George to pho again today
to find out how they are - they bring

you up. they love you *so so so* much
my darling - who shd have gone be-
fore you - their voices even in that
far-off phone - they haunt me w/the-
ir love inconsolation sorrow - **she
tek a 'turn' George say Time say &
even now her eyes are red & fat w/
weepin**. . .

two

Aunt Lucille

We too have shared her admonitions
have looked on her with something of respect
until the vegetable years

demanding deeper roots
a harder covering
beyond her soft commandering

have fashioned her
into a symbol into a silent smile
guarding the garden

. and deserted and growing apart . have made of her worries .
a hand sliding over the fur
of our wild unaccountable lies

Elegy for Rosita

That she is suddenly still
with her stillness her mourning
i cannot think

i cannot know
the anxious pilgrimage of blood
that only finds a doctor's watered consolation
and so returns in crisis to the helpless life
brinked on the precipice of her heart's rending

That she is suddenly come
to the door of her pain's ending
i cannot think

Nor can i pray that morning will
not raise the mourning from her head
nor hoist the suns back to her eyes

to say she is not dead

Cambridge
Oct 1951 rev CowPastor 28 Dec 98 12 feb 90 . for Richard Clarke

12

Circle(s)

for
Melba Liston & Marjorie Whylie

Music will never fly out of your green horn in squares
nor out of your harp nor out of your thumb pianos

because it does not grow on cottonwool plantations
it is not manufractured goods nor made of metal neither

it can never go straight up to heaven
clambering up its notes from a ladder in the sky

for it curls like your hair around its alabama root . ripples
like fishwater around your children's sticks

has deep watery eyes like a sea lion . has clear fiery eyes like a hawk
it sees through stone . and dynamites itself in chalky quarries

of deep bone . bringin our riddim home
it is the blue lagoon inside your slide trombone

it is the echo not the rock that does
it.   it is that reggae reggae riddim that Xplodes the prison burns the clock

Harlem

for
Myrna Bain

O Myrna Bain
so bright the bronze so brave the sybil warrieuse
so clear & consonant the syllables

so clearly gone us now
the rain
the dorothea administring to you

the last rites of the killers of yr pain
dressed now in white so you are comforted. soft now
after such storms & hurricanes

this harlem harbour nr st nicholas where you sail lately yr life on
shipwrecked and drifted sometimes. stayed
however. prayed every ómò obosom our better future

And yet you were neglected
loved more than you had love and luck
wd have it so. yr back unwanting pocket for the orphanage

Now you will always walk with us along the black
beach of the shadow of the south coast crater of Jamaica
marvelling at magmamatic pebbles

and the laterite that fall there long ago
before the green before the time of canes before the flame
that come to torture & consume from yr appeal

the sweet & clamour of the pealing bells
that take yr hair & tear
it. destroy that lion voice so that it seem not even fire-

moths aglow wd fear it. the wound you bear inside
you folded flared and so unhealing feeling
that you begin to fade

away from sun. light lacking like yr shadow in the hall-
way down the wide brownstone steps around the grill-
work & the aspen at the corner standing in its shade

until you knew you cd not even walk where once yr soul
so brightly laugh aloud & talk to alice coltrane rosa guy the eldren
garvey neighbours by the minton jazz-club and the laundrymat

the herbalist still sellin ole newspapers secrets sucrets darlin
mists & juices round the block
O let it knit back now o silent rose o blossom of this cloud-

(y) afternoon. a walk w/you across the lawn to sit the visit
in a quiet garden tuck below the close & boarded rooms & flats
for sale. though these were not the images you choose -

the shattered street the stone the bare neglecting statuettes
the ghetto slowly blinding you
the easy life of lights & wife you not unlightly have refuse

Duke

for Anne Walmsley

●

The old man's hands are alligator
skins
and swimming easily like these
along the harp stringed keyboard
where he will make
of
Solitude
a silver thing

as if great age like his
could play that tune along
these cracks that flow
between their swing
without a scratch of thistle
sound
& whistle down the rhythm all wing long
&

what a way to love you madly madly madly
with the wisdom of so many
all night carioca smokes
& dish & clutter knife & clatter up the baad bo
diddley dancehall bars & barrios

·

my Cousin Bigard

ing in the piss stain

RESTROOMS

mood & oboe
indigo

·

wet glass

of

SUPA
NOVA HEADLIGHTS

Ç

Bessie
Bessie
Bessie Smith
the empress of our shattered blues

&
you
smiling up front in the coach every morning
after the thousand &
one
one night stands

Watts
St Louis
Selma Alabama
Chicago
Montgomery
Bus Boycott
Cairo
where they most nearly kill you
Sphinx
Pharaoh
Memphis Tennessee

where they did where they did
where they finally did

but
the happy-go-lucky-locals
shout. in
out

run Jesse run
Jesse run Jesse
run

call yo out
cast . low
down
you caint make

it
you're nothin . you're from no
body
3rd class servant class got-no-class underclass

it is not a question my friends
about a telephone call
of who tango with who
of who shit. in with who in the shithouse

is a matter of hope of the right to continue the dream
about our rightful place at the table

&

the curtain psyching up
& the lights swimming down into the thunder of silence

& each time each time is that creak before birth
Jimmy Hamilton's like carolina clarinet
leading us out of the silence

•

Afternoon of a saxophone
Caravan
Perdido
Cottontail
Satin Doll
Sophisticated Lady
Transblucency
the creo
Creole Love Call

&

Let me hear it one more time

for

IVIE ANDERSONNNG

&

DC
in summer
hot almost too simmer to sip . sop sit out on the stoep
with old men . cymbell children

cries rising like these northern egrets
above the railway tracks
where Sonny Greer come walk
ing down the sidewalk clickin sticks

•

the ole man plays the tune
with ancient hands of jungle tints
of stride piano at the Cotton Club
New Orleans woman drum

Gonsalves
Rabbit
Harry Carney
Cootie
Nanton
Woodyard
Blanton
Cat
the
doo-doo doo-doo wah
of
Harlem Air-Shaft

warm & deep where i am born upon the sidewalk
on the corner . in the precinct with no father to my name . no name
but what my grannma give me

our mother dragging us across
the midnight city looking for a place to sleep
at least to keep her box of broken winnings in. takin two jobs
like twins

so she could feed us chicken bone
to keep our hopes alive
an not a one a we she always say *too poor*
to hear a pride a **Ko-Ko** *trombone lion roar*

•

the ole man's hands are striding through
the keyboard sidewalks alleyways & ages

from
Shakka speare and guinea birD

to
Caribbean stilt dance

vèvè
masquerade

&
Buddy Bolden's golden Strayhorn horn across the misty
goombay levee dawn
that no cheap jazzhouse perfume scent can cheapen

•

his hands are playing every Tricky Nantam book in town
black black Black Bottom Stomp
diminuendo honey beige & hallelujah brown

·

& look
the old man's alligator hands are young

tree

mesongs

I

Those who i hold most dear
are nvr dead

they become more than fixed
in song or stone or album

mixed with my sand and mortar
they walk in me with the world

II

How often have we stood
sombred in mourning
scattering dust to dust & ashes

to the earth. the flowers wilt re-
cover with the rain and re-
wither. petals colours into dust

But in our house
behind our words our wines
the flowers bloom are free for-
ever and again the dead dust shines with us
in the completed silence

III

The dancer dance to death
but we only know the dancing

the strings the joints the places
to be oiled the rust after the last
performance are denied to us

we only know the dancing

IV

My dog died in the night
we find him
cold & ugly
early that morning
the flies already at his mouth

in the green jumping water
in a sack
they have thrown him overboard
at a spot where the land lies low
and the sky is big & blue

but he
my poor dog dead
was bigger than the bay and the blue sky
his bark was sharper than sharks
his tale was all animals

for he
my poor dog dead
was sun song stone statue

my loved ones

▼
for Elizabeth Schepky

Have you been here? this vase
of flowers reassures me. they
cut daffodils. create their yellow sky
their green plantations in the water there

soon they will droop. their wild bells withered
their straight stalks xclamations slipped into a question mark. this
death have you created
when out of the blue the brightest day of the year

your hands placed them. the art of the daffodils. there

VI

Even your letters

though they
attempting to be living
shatter the glass

the spent fragments
mirror the cracked colossus
the attempted life

even your letters

the sent silver
the brittle breaking present
glimpses & glimmers your love

the constellations

VII

There are no murmurs in the mind
talk. like the poles. is fixed
a voice made visible
and a thousand situations spin
into the complexity of simpleness
there is no movement in the fire
a silence glows like music in the lyre

VIII

Now you will come to me
imagination is the stretch of strings
on which your newness ever enters
like the light

you will be brightly burning
like the child the flower
the wild wet winging out of shower
the sudden sunlight flashing from the spire

a silence glows like music from the fire

IX

So cruel is creating
it must be killing to be keeping

must be the song beyond the passion
the cup beyond the potter's wheel

not the wonderful face in the mirror
but the flowerfall under the pool

we little guessed this raphael
was yesterday a baker's girl

with flowers in her hair
or that icarus was dying in air

X

Sleep now my darling

your hair hush as fields
eyelids like morning windowpanes
let not the wheel of birds
coerce you from the stillness

this touch would ring your flesh

XI

Unhappily for Goliath
you will never fling that stone
this Moses will be forever conquer-
ing . and i forever listening
will have you ever always coming to me up the stair-
way(s) . the possibility of song

XII

We the creators must be forever cruel
the hair we brush
dies . the river
dries out of its flowing

this bird will be forever. never going
we smash the mirror . break the glass
between one world and tomorrow
find love perfected in the rustle fire

We the creators must be forever cruel
seeking to restore the Holy Grail. the assoon lwa. the
unxampled look .   the white bright moment of the miracle

XIII

While he wrestle through seasons
with sun stone wind
he stored the real the true creation
in his mind. saw sea sun stone
become the dream the un. touch(ed) bone

XIV

The play dull the stage dark
actors dwarfed by the words
till someone drew a sword
and the steel was there. near me
on the wall . and i was play and player and poet and all

XV

His pain climbing beyond the height of eagles
flashed in the noon beaks & wild wings

he taloned music from the dark
achieving after seasons

the swimmer the diver the dancer
the runner the river the rain

XVI
for Elizabeth Schepky

She draw the bow across the strings
diverting the whole world to silence
music the room her wrist across the strings
converted the forever
making of us. black white Italian Japanese and Jew
a blossom(ed) flower

XVII

Only in little children
are the words and the wonder alike

he softly say Maria

and see her in his brown eyes coming
his mother the virgin his marvellous art

XVIII

To burn to blaze to lose the sense of time
to flower like the flame into simplicity
to be the moment when the razor hurts
the carnival balloons big till they burst

XIX

In early summer in the woods
the ecstasy is not alone in branch or flower
but in the white twined two by the pool
her fingers in his shirt on his lightning flesh

XX

Clash clapping to castanets
they climb the tangô
into unclipp(ed) freedom

so feel perfection flood
the blood they dance

beyond their bodies' dark delirium
they find clear flight. annihilation

XXI
Day at Devizes (I)

Spires hoist hearts high

but city blocks against the sky
are heavy. push our hopes back

down to the basement

xistence is the butterfly in flight
feeling along its flickering light

the whole world weighting

XXII
Day at Devizes (2)

How green the air is
wrapped in wind shawls
how moth the cool is

how infant the sky is
blue egg along white wall
how cool the height is

how star the breeze is
twinkled with wood bird calls
how born the spring is

XXIII
for Barbara on The Backs at Cambridge before i meet her

Stranger who reeds

goldenly her gold book
under her gold hair

in weaving the web
of the day's equil-
ibrium's complete-

ly involved in the still
of her sitting's x-
citement

you feel her balance(d)
against you
whose moving away

is like falling through
sitting the sitter x-
pected was there

XXIV
for Barbara at Devizes

And suddenly you was talking trees
fall black with birds behind the hill
and green as grass fly off
into the sun o blinding girl
the whole cathedral crash at your back

XXV

Not the blue the orthodoxy of the day
But a blue like intuition
The soft of the night into morning
Felt here . remembered
Under the hoofs of the cart

XXVI

i have created this room. it is my world
you shared in it the flowers. but now you have
left me alone

and this is my room. the chair
the folded cheese-coloured blanket
the books silent as centuries

even the sensational sky. today. is part of my room
and i shall sit on until steps. creaking the stairs
come bringing the dust from the kingdom

XXVII

Happy now? i shall show
you my photograph album

This was the day when i cut my finger
there was a tall man on bumbatuk stilts
and a ragged man glowing to drums
when the painful red wet running
went down the pink shells and the vivid sand

My eyes were filled with bright young worlds
and i could hardly see
the ragged man and the tall man on stilts

But the blood there blazed
and i hear(d) the rush of the white sea horses
till the air pulled tight as drums
over the ragged man and the sudden silence tall as stilts

XXVIII
At the death of a young poet's wife
for Erika Ritter . *La Bohème à Paris 1898*

And it was fitting that he should have notice first

he who had seen so much in people
that he acted out their lives before his friends

he with such warmth within him
that he lighted up the house when he come in
it was fitting that an actor should have notice first

the others move about the room. around the table
stood waiting by the fire. arrange things
on the mantelpiece. picked up a vase and put it back again
a painter. a musician. helpless friends

you waited for the doctor. move quickly to the door
and throw it open. hoping against all hope
to find him standing on the mat

outside. to hear his footsteps on the stair. the hall
door open . slam
yr listening stood lonely opening far

doors. then you move slowly to the window. lean
wishes out. the street was empty. not a sight
nor sound. so softly draw the curtains. turn
-ing back into the darken room. a helpless poet

and he had seen already. he who was fitted to have seen
so much. appearing casually to cross the room
he knew it all along. went still to look
but could not act before his friends what he now saw

so stood in silence. helpless actor
lost of all comedy. learning a gesture from her
that he had not known before

O could the painter paint this scene
he who could carry in his fingers' diligence
green. sky. the crowded walks and alleys
of his curiosity. child flower girl

the smile the market-scene the carnival the queen
and w/his brush and pencil restore them to forever life
could he command perspectives now?

He turned

he saw the actor in his attitude
he saw the girl. the endless silence stretching out
between him and her lines her curve her colour. the three
dimensions of her getting empty

. and there they stood. player and painter placed
before this girl who was not raw material now
but artifact. lips lids leaves of her hair

all fallen in a fine perfection. only remains
for him who spins his silver web of counterpain
from air. to catch her pitch and silence

A requiem. a mass that would rise up from darkness
like a single vase in its complexity of lutes and strings
a patient web of singing love that would connect the room
crisscross of fugue that would offset the coming dust

a lonely violin. a heartbreak harp. but turning
the musician only heard the splintering vase
only the breaking web. the snapping strings
and beyond. a silence that restores them all

And so when you turn back from window's
hope. you find a finish room. three friends
the daily labour of their loves performed. only your lover
lying there was like a sorrow you had hope

postpone. You went to them. their standing fascinated you
you wanted words from them but find they could not speak
you turn to her. her stillness fascinating you
you wanted words from her but found she could not speak
you wanted words for words were life to you

words to assuage the silence that you could not understand
words to refashion futures like a healer's hand
words that would walk long down the dark steps of beyond
her bed. calling the gone-away the light the open door
the path of words from darkness that would have brought her back

And there you stood. lost beyond metaphors in search
song gesture colour act. one word
wd too distract the faith that followed you and fall
and be consumed w/in the depthless silence of her death

XXIX

So cruel is creating
it must be killing to be keeping

must be the song beyond the passion
the cup beyond the potter's wheel

not the wonderful face in the mirror
but narcissus under the pool

we little guessed this raphael
was yesterday a baker's girl

with falling flowers in her hair
or that icarus was dying in air

four

Letter to
Zea Mexican

(2)

And you my love? Can you see me?
Hear me? Are you close by? Angry?
Frustrated? Relieved? Delighted?
Amused? Sorry? Puzzled? Lonely?
Far-a-way? Desolate? Indifferent?
Different? The same? Changing?
And if so, how? Do I affect you? Do
you affect me? Us? Are you happy
or still suffering? What is it like &
how is it w/you across the water/or is
there nothing nothing nothing at all
as I think you xpected as I think yu
sometimes say tho I not too too sure
about that At least you always say
yu try to **philosophical** about it -
death & dying - *and tho you wish yr bo-*
dy to be burn - yu nvr even tell me th-
at. since i cd not discuss this. see
this. imagine yu not here - and so
yu must have tell my sister - **burn** . .

but from the poems that yu love &
cd quote about the **cosmos**. . . and fro
(m) the way you kneel at church - so
deep attentive - as if yu wheeling
silent into Word - I know you feel
there's something more some some->
thing much much more to make it
all worthwhile & you were also very
strong on *retribution* (yu felt at least it
ought to *happen* - some kinda **pay**. *back*
some *where!*) - & wonder why it seem <
the **good** get often nothing. . .

48

Miss Mac has turn all the beds out
and yr chairs over up at Irish Tn *so*
that you won't come back for goodness
sake! *to harm us!!* Can you imagine
that! The wisdom of the folk I love!
When all I want is have you back!
Beyond all words I want to have you
back. But now dem seh yu diffrent
now. that if i leave yr clothes yr clo-
thes. yr chair yr chair. yr bed our be
(d). you'll come back in. lie down in
bed beside me and want me *foop* you
like before. Thats what dem tell me
And it cyaant be so dem tell me. As
if you cross some Great Divine Div-
ide or Water and you of all people
my love are now some Something
Dangerous & Other - some somethin
(g) Different & Alien & even Ugly.
Can you imagine how this make me feel?
Jean makes me sleep on only blue
sheets now and places nutmeg under
neath my pillow My sister Mary sp-
eaks about **'A Great Cloud of Wit-
nesses'** whatever that may mean - th-
at further frightens & dis. tresses me
I suppose dem don't even want you
to **Go & be a Beneficent Spirit &
Come to us in the Morning** as I say
in the poem you ask me to read for
you from **Islands** & which Mary ree
(d) at yr Thanksgiving Service at
Mona & the Congo Square Writers
(Tom Dent & dem in New Orleans) send a
>>>>>loving cable quoting from<<<<<
Mother Poem

She is alpha
is omega she is happy
<< . >>

I hope so love. You **deserve** it. if I <
may put it this way. Yu deserve the
best the best the best there is mek I <
tell yu. And all the letters that have
come have join this growing chorus
>**Doris was gold/Doris is gold**< <
from Ramases of all people . but I bl-
ess him for it for is true - in all yr na.
mes. remember?

And yet have I 'blasphemed' against
you - because I love you so so utter-
ly/securely like John Figueroa say-
ing once how good Catholics cd aff-
ord to criticize their Church because
they love the Madre & she is big &
broad enough t'include them in its
faith & fruits & even in their curses
So that you give me the energy even
to be 'unfaithful' tho I was never that
sharing the munificence you gave to
me w/others tho it was that/was not
that either/but it must have hurt/yu
always said is something that you >
cdnt understand

What worries me *(is too late now)* is
that I don't know how/how far & dee
ply down it hit you hit you hurt you
. . .and if this cause the cancer. . .

And me? In the first place I can't im-
agine life & love w/out yu out/yu ou
(t)/yu Can't see how I'll manage nei
ther. Lovers muses girl-frenns help-
ers will nvr be enuff & cannot be// &
I have to be beware of frittering the
energy of gettin too involve in thing
(s) I won't be able get out of - as you
have warn me many times about - dang-
ers & even ᴠoıᴏᴌᴇᴎᴄᴇ as a result of
such entanglement(s). my own bad
look. bad luck. the need of what my
Mother once call *circumspection* & i as
(k) yu now to stand beside me stand
up in fact **in front of me** to comfort &
forgive me

Now you have gone into that light
of which you were always a part
Every one speaks of yr radiance
This man proud of yu Zea Mexican
as he is from
the very beginning when you first
walk towards me at that dance
at NormaForde & KP notice
but nvr more so than the day I take
you home to RoundHouse
and Mile&Quarter & the ancestors
evvabody from Mother to Joan
& John & all the aunts & uncles
& St Elmo i remember & Richard
& Myrtle & Francina
& Cyril & Queen Victoria
(tho Bob'ob was gone
& Uncle Lawson)

& KP of course & KP's Mama Pile
& we get the blessing of Esse

- really a whole Cloud Of Witnesses! -

come to me as if in **shock**
& **yes yes yes yes yes yes yes**
She is the one She is the wonderful -
my lady of the golden warakuna skin
my tê my tê my Tetêmexticantl

five

Cherries

for Odale

So when the hammers of the witnesses of heaven are raise all together up

yonder. there will be dumbness in the choir tonight

when the voices are raise all together
black kites flying on what should be a holiday

there will be silence in the cathedral

a woman love a man
she will lick the sweat from his forehead

she will walk miles to see im
and wait for him by the corner

she will bear his children loudly

upon the earth is firm foot
toes searching the top-

soil gripping

the instep. the angles of knub. ankle & heel
are grey w/the roads

w/the long hypodermics of noon

.

the dress tucks itself over the black buttocks
into the suction of thighs. the hip
is a scythe

grass growling along the hill-
side. she will bend forward w/the hoe. *huh*
and the gravel will answer her. *so*

she will swing upward w/the hoe. *huh*
and the bones of the plantation will come ringing to meet her. *so*
her sweat will water the onions & the shaddock & the wild thyme

she will bear his children proudly

.

but when he turns sour
on her. scowling. wiping her face with his anger
stiffening his spine beside her on the bed. not

caressing her curves w/eye-
lash or word or jook
of the elbow. she will curdle like milk

the bones of the plantation will come ringing to meet her. *so*
the bucket will rattle in the morning at the stannpipe
but there will be no water

the skillet will rattle at midday
but there will be no milk
she will become the mother of bastards

.

when the hammers are raise all together
rows of iron teeth swinging down. *huh*
there will be dumbness in the choir tonight

when the voices are raise all together
black fists gathering storm on what is not
a holiday.   there will be silence in the cathedral

the light will fall through pains of glass
on broken stone.   on steps that can go no
father.   on love alive bleeding on its thorns

when a woman love a man
when a man naddent

> *if there are ways of saying yes*
> *i do not know them*

> *if there are dreams*
> *i cannot recall them to the light*

> *if there is rage*
> *it is a cool cinder*

in the heat of the day
i swear i will sweat no more

knife. bill-hook. sweet bramble
i will burn in my bush of screams

hoe. *i will work*
    root. mud. marl. burden

needle. *i will sew*
    thread. stitch. embroideried image

jesus. *i will serve thee*
       knee. copper. rain falling from heaviest heaven
       of storm

but i will drink you no more
torch you no more
sweaten you out on the lumps of the mattrass no longer

the hoe will stand in the corner by the backdoor
cane flowers will flicker w/rainflies
but there will be no crop-over songs

the fields will grow green soundlessly
the roots will ribbon until they burst
and then they will ribbon again until they burst

but there will be no kukoo or okro or jugg .
the needle will grow rusty in the cloth .
pin. pinch of thread. thimble

it will make no silver track & tremble far into the night
no dress will take shape over my head
slipping down like water over my naked breasts

the seats of the chapel will remain empty
the wicks burning at altar until daybreak
fatten by shadows and moths

   .

yr foetus i will poison
dark dark mollusc
spinach susum suck-de-well-dry bush

the child still fish.   still lizard
wrinkled gill & croaking gizzard
i will destroy

blinding the eyeballs
pulling out the flag of its tongue by the shreddards
ripping open the egg of its skull w/sunless manchioneal blisters

i will carry the wet twitching rag
bearing your face. conveying your futureless race
in its burst bag of balls to your doorstep

maaaa   it will cry
& the windows will be pulled down tight against the wind
meeowww   it will howl

      & a black dog will go prowling past the dripping pit latrines

       & when the moon is a wild flower falling through cloud
          from patch to shade you will see it

        once our child our toil of touch our sharing
     sitting under the sandbox tree. smiling. smiling. smiling

        slipping its plate of bleed

          -

       these images of love i leave you
        now i no longer need you

       man . manwaart . manimal

Poem for Walter Rodney

assassinated Georgetown Guyana 13 June 1980.   the poem thinking also of Pat Rodney and the children

I

to be blown into fragments. your flesh
like the islands that you love
like the seawall that you wish to heal

bringing equal rights & justice to the brothers
a fearless cumfa mashramani to the sisters
whispering their free/zon . that grandee nanny's histories be listen

to with all their ancient flèch. es of respect
until they are the steps up the poor of the church
up from the floor of the hill/slide
until they become the roar of the nation

that fathers would at last settle into what they own
axe adze if not oil-well. torch-
light of mackenzie

that those who have all these generations
bitten us bare to the bone
gnawing our knuckles to the quick

price fix. price rise. rachman and rat-
chet squeeze
how bread is hard to buy how rice

is scarcer than the muddy water where it rides
how bonny baby bellies grow
noom-laaden dungeon grounded down

to groaning in their hunger. grow
wailer-voiced & red-eyed w/out sunlight in their anger
that knocks against their xylophones of prison ribs and bars

that how we cannot take our wives or sweethearts
or our children or our children's chilldren
on a trip to kenya. watch

maasai signal from their saffron shadow
the waterbuck and giraffe wheel round wrecked manyatta
while little blonder kinter who don't even care

a fart. for whom this is the one more yard
a flim. for whom this is the one more start
to colon to cortes to cecil rhodes

to whom this is the one more road
to the thathi-headed waiter aban/died out of his shit by his baas at the nairobi
airport hotel

lets his face sulk into i soup
lets his hairshirt wrackle i sweat
cause i man am wearing the tam of i dream in i head

that these and those who fly still dread/er up the sky
vultures & hawks. eye
scarpering morgan the mi/ami mogul

those night beasts a babylon who heiss us on sus
but that worst it is the blink
in iani own eye. the sun blott-

ed out by paper a cane fires vamp/ires
a ink wheels emp/ires a status quos a status quos a status crows
that tell a blood toll/ing in the ghetto

till these small miss/demeanours as you call them
be-
come a monstrous fetter on the land that will not let us breed

until every chupse in the face of good morning
be-
come one more coil one more spring one more no-

thing to sing/about
be-
come the boulder rising in the bleed

the shoulder nourishing the gun
the headlines screaming of the skrawl across the wall
of surbiton of sheraton hotel

dat **POR OYAAAN TEK NO MOORE**

and the babies and their mothers and their mothers
and their mothers and their mothers mothers
and their mothers mothers mothers mothers

perishing forever in the semi-automatic catcalls of the orange heat & sizzle fear
& flare-up of the siren
howl of the scorch wind wail through the rat-a-tat

of the hool
through the tap of your head. damp. stench. criall
the well of flame drilling through your flesh

reduced to the time before green/bone
reduced to the time before ash/skull
reduced to the time before love/was born

in your arms
before dawn was torn from your pillow

in your arms
before the tumours were crumpled into paper bags
inside the star. broek market

in your arms
before the knife run through the dark
and locket steel was there between the spine and kidney

in your arms
in your arms
in your arms

i prophesay
before you recognize the gorgon head inside the red
eye of the walkie-talkie

♟
to be blown into fragments. your death

like the islands that you love
like the seawall that you wish
to heal. bringing equal rights and justice to the brothers

that children above all others would be like the sun-
rise over the rupunnunni over the hazy morne over kilimanjaro
any where or world where there is love

there is the sky and its blue
free. where past means present struggle
towards vlissingens where it may some day end

distant like powis on the essequibo
drifting like miracles or dream
or like that lonely fishing engine slowly losing us its sound

but real like your wrist with its tick of blood
over its man. acles of bone
but real like the long marches. the court steps of trial

the sodden night journeys holed up in a different safe house
every morning. and trying to guess from the heat
of the hand-

shake if stranger was stranger or cobra or friend
and the urgent steel of the kiskadee glittering its *qqurl*
down the sharpest bend in the breeze and the leaves ticking

and learning to live with the smell of rum on the skull's
breath. his cigarette ash
on the smudge of your fingers. his footsteps

into your houses

and having to say it over and over and over again
with your soft ringing patience with your black-
lash of wit. tho the edges must have been curling with pain

but the certainty clearer and clearer and clearer again   .
that it must be too simple to hit
too hurt/not to remember

that it must not become an easy slogan or target
too torn too defaced too devalued
down in redemption market

that when men gather govern other manner
they should be honest in a world of hornets
that bleed into their heads like lice

corruption that cockroaches like a dirty kitchen sink .
that politics should be like understanding.of the floorboards
of your house swept clean each morning

built by hands that know the wind and tide and language
from the loops within the ridges of your footprints
to the rusty tinnin fences of your yard

•

so that each man on his cramped restless island
on his back. dam of land in forest clearing by the broeken
river. where berbice struggles against slushy ground

takes up his bed and walk

in the power and the reggae of his soul/stice
from the crippled brambled pathways of his vision
to the certain limpen knowledge of his **nam**

3
this is the message that the idren will deliver
grounded with drift of mustard seed

that when he spoke the word was fluter on his breeze
since it was natural to him like the way he listen

like the way he walk
one of those ital brothers who have grace

for being all these things and careful of it too
and careless of it too

he was cut down plantation cane
because he dared to grow and growing. green

because he was that slender reed
and there were machetes sharp enough to hasten it and bleed

he was blown down
because his bridge from man to men mean

doom to prisons of a world we never made
meant wracking out the weeds that rake we yampe vine

•
And so the bomb
fragmenting islands like the land we love
letting back darkness in

•
But there are stars that burn that murders do not know
soft diamonds behind the blown to bits
that trackers could not find that bombers could not see

that scavengers will never hide away
the caribbean bleeds near georgetown prison
a widow rushes out . and hauls her children free

started in London June 1980 on hearing the news . first pub Race Today Review (1980/81) & in Third World Poems (1983)

for Mikey Smith
stone to death on Stony Hill Kingston Jamaica on Marcus Garvey birtday 17 August 1983

When the stone fall that morning out of the johncrow sky
it was not dark at first . that opening on to the red sea humming
but something in my mouth like feathers . blue like bubbles
carrying signals & planets & the sliding curve of the world like a water pic
-ture in a raindrop when the pressure. drop

When the stone fall that morning out of the johncrow sky
i couldn't cry out because my mouth was full of beast & plunder
as if i was gnashing badwords among tombstones
as if that road up stony hill . round the bend by the church

-yard . on the way to the post office . was a bad bad dream
and the dream was like a snarl of broken copper wire zig zagg
-in its electric flashes up the hill & splitt. in spark & flow
-ers high. er up the hill . past the white houses & the ogogs bark

-ing all teeth & fur. nace & my mother like she up . like she up . like she up
-side down up a tree like she was scream. like she was scream. ing no & no
-body i could hear could hear a word i say. in . even though
they was so many poems left & the tape was switch on & runn. ing &

runn. ing & the green light was red & they was stannin up there & evva. where
in london & amsterdam & at unesco in paris & in west berlin
& clapp. in & clapp. in & clapp. in & not a soul on stony hill to even say amen
. an yet it was happening happening happening . the fences begin

to crack in i skull . and there was a loud **boodooooooooooooooooooogs**
like guns goin off . dem ole-time magnums . or like a fireworks of dreadlocks
was on fire . and the gaps whe the river comin down inna the drei gully
where my teeth use to be smilin . an i tuff gong tong

that use to press against them & parade pronunciation . now unannounce
an like a black wick in i head & dead . &
it was like a heavy heavy riddim low down in i belly . bleedin dub . &
there was like this heavy heavy black dog tump. ing in i chest & pump. ing

murderrrrrrrrrrrrrrrrrrrrrrrrrrrrrrrrrrrrrrrrrrrrrrrrrrrrrrrrrrrrrrrrrrrrrrrrr

& i throat like dem tie. like dem tie. like dem tie a tight tie around
it. twist. ing my name quick crick . quick crick . an a nvva wear neck

-tie yet . an a hear when de big boot kick down i door . stump
-in it foot pun a knot in de floor. board . a window slam shat at de back
a mi heart . de itch & oooze & damp a de yaaad in my silver tam

-bourines closer & closer . st joseph marching bands crash
-ing & closer
& *bom si. cai si. ca* boom ship bell . *nom si. cai si ca* boom ship bell

& a laughin more blood
& spittin out

lꞏ▬▬▬▬▬▬▬▬▬▬▬▬▬▬▬▬▬▬▬▬▬▬▬▬▬▬▬▬▬▬▬▬▬◢

i two eye lock to the sun & the two sun starin back black from de grass
& a bline to de butterfly fly

-in

•

& it was like a wave on stony hill caught in a crust of sun
-light

•

& it was like a matchstick schooner into harbour
muffled in the silence of it wound

•

& it was like the blue of speace was filling up the heavens with it thunder
& it was like the wind was grow. in skin

•

the skin have hard ears . hardering

•

& it was like marcus garvey rising from his coin . steppin towards his people
cryin dark

& every mighty word he trod . the ground fall dark & hole be
-hine him like it was a bloom x. plodin sound . my ears was bleed

-in sounn-

•

& i am quiet now because i have become that sounn
the sun. light morning wash the choral limestone harsh

against the soft volcanic ash. *i was*
& it was slippin past me into water & it was
slippin pass me into root. *i was*

& it was
slippin pass me into flower. & it was
ripping upwards into shoot. *i was*

& every politrician tongue in town was lash
-in me w/spit & cut. rass wit & ivy whip & wrinkle jumbimum
it was like warthog . grunt

-ing in the grounnn

& chilldren running down the hill run right on through the splash
of pouis that my breathe. ing make when it was howl & red & bubble

& sparrow twits pluck tic & tap. worm from the grass
as if i man did nvva have no face . as if i man did nvva in dis place

•

When the stone fall that morning out of the johncrow sky
i could not hold it brack or black it back or block it off or limp
away or roll it from me into memory or light or rock it steady into night. be-

cause it builds me now w/leaf & spiderweb & soft & crunch
& like the powderwhite & slip & grit inside your leather. boot & fills my blood
w/deaf my bone w/hobble dumb & echo. less neglect neglect neglect neglect

&

i▬▬▬▬▬▬▬▬▬▬▬▬▬▬▬▬▬▬▬▬▬▬▬▬▬▬▬▬▬▬▬▬▬▬▬▬d

•

i am the stone that kills me

Défilée

for Joan Dayan & Ezili Dantô

About noon on friday October 17 1806 not three years after he was declared/declared
himself Head of State & Emperor . Jean Jacques Dessalines the Liberator of Haiti
successor of Toussaint Legba Louverture
was assassinated by soldiers from the South on the road from Marchand
two miles to Port-au-Prince the capital. His shot & stabb-up body was stoned & torn
to pieces by his murderers & left. it is said. to be found & taken for burial
by the 'madwoman' Défilée. a meat seller (vivandière) reputedly once the Emperor's lover

*B*right thrones have been cast down before
the leaders stripped & torn from power. fled
or dead. Dessalines my liberator my xecutioner

mon Empereur

my lover of Pont-Rouge like this
who break the bread w/bloody hands who tear
the nation flag at Lakayè & make it red

& make it blue. unfurl it new . where now it stands
for slave & bloody cloth & resurrected
nèg. who stone the whiteman down

from im goliam towerhome at Cormiers
. Verrettes . the crackle battleaxe of musketeers
against La Crête

Now here w/out yr head w/out yr virile hands. be
-reft of Claire Heureuse. of balls. bereft of eyes
yr ears cut off from music. matross. cannon
. chasseurs ak racheteers

                    the tendresse of yr up. full spirit
                  . pull down in. to this mud where no
                  clouds move across the sky where no

                  stars stare where no wind blues where no
          sun shines upon yr skin. where the red blood un
          -gurgle from yr throat now flows & flowers

                                        flowers

                          O Dessalines so so cut up
                        O splendid coat so splendidly
                                        cut down

        cows on this dry pasture all my strife
        provide me meat. goats. blackbelly sheep are here
        hens. turncoat & turkeycocks jack rabbits rare
        but sweet swift bones so wash-away w/life

        each morning to yr door i bring this little covered
        heap of nyampe victuals. the long dark face i so adore
        the fingers in the plate the morsel to your lips
        my love my pain. plain sacrifice

        my sweet flesh on yr palate my plasaj
        O salvage
        warrior o how you chop me up you chop me
        down into the howling hot prostrations

        of yr love
        O how i love
        each shaken silken golden moment of yr power

Now in this coarse pig-stain macoute
i carry w/me everywhere for years
. it watch my rape. witness

my parents death. how Rochambeau come kill
down all my breddas and my two only suns
inside the Cahos mountains. trick Toussaint off

to France till i go mad w/all this blood
this trekking death down in this mud
betrayals

maroon dark nights
mornings of rendezvous
quick anxious crossing of the river coming back to you

mules on the edges of high trails of mountain passes
my mind cooing w/in the mourn of woodoves morn-
ing long . witchering myself like blackbirds on the floor

criss-crossing imperfections in myself made mad
w/manananse working working working cross
the star . bed straw . bed ceiling of my floor

Now sit i down beside you in yr pool of blood
w/seven wailer demons in my head. poor fool
to let them fling you down like this from yr high

horse. yr vision of a people marching on
out of this dungeon hearse of slavery into some proper light
no blight no more upon this twisted crop of niggers on the land

po fou they cut you down before the morning crow
before the crowd that might have save you
gather on the road from Marèchand two
miles to Port-au-Prince

the meat they make of you i cannot sell
tho i sell sutler meat at Ogoum all my life
the fragments of yr body's dream i can but touch
O cruel piece by piece i can but gather

from the entrail entrance of the knife .
there's no peace here. gape-
ing & gashes like hot milk boil-
ing over & the furnace burn-

ing our tomorrows spoil our race .
Duclos my love i cannot find yr face
this is yr head wuhloss my love
how tenderly i love these harsh Dahomey

scars. the whipmarks on yr back. the prison bars
you break w/these once hands from which you
flame. is this one eye of moon i find
wrapped in the grass of years?

i cannot find the tongue you kiss me with & spit
me wit. and when you spurn me. turn me out .
i sit down at yr door & wait for morning take me
down to Fort St-Clair . or bring me bask

into the bed & spur & task of you . this lip
torn from yr skull i find near clammacherry
bushes here. its strip of skin still living so it
seem to sneer where it shd smile

mile after mile i walk
w/you mile after mile i walk
for you mile after mile i fight i hurt i heal O ride
Arada ride. this is your angle bone

this is yr broeken hand the ruby ring still blinking
on yr flinger O this can this can never be. how they
dis- member dis. honour dis. remember you.
assoun
my bell my open door my lover

             And so i pick you back each pick & pluck
                     a root a memory a wake a flower
                 the toes back to the fit of instep & the ball
                         -bearing weight of ankle

                     -bone. let the one foot if it be one
                         foot walk quickly down the road
                 let the slip hips dance. fit fairly into place
                             around the ready loins

                     let us make love again & laugh
                 the belly here the guts . the navel strings
                         the high kite of the angel noom
remembering yr ancestors yr élevé mapou estate mi moun

assemble me yr lungs again so you may breathe
& shout commands. turn the horse round
& gallop off to victory at Miragoame & Vertières

let me ride with you général. let me ride with you
. in these dark eyes i will restore our ayisyen
in this fine head i plant here in this place of burial

O Papa Dessalines O JanJak Desalin Gangan
O magic makandal & carrefô & sun & flag
plaçage & nanciòn

Xangô
at the Summer Solstice
for Oya. in Washington sQ. Park. Manhattan

ângo cyaan go no far

-tha. all winter long he store the sounds you hear
now in these man
-dolins. all through the cold hard dark he labour

for this light
& now he find it on im lip. e blow the flute
e string the lute . im rise & go again

lookin for his Oya of the after
-noon . im rose im pain the pale flame of im sun
-set in the western tree

She sits now in the harmattan. surrendering
to all this wave
-ing green . heed

-less of headlong papers todlers marijuana pushers lovers
she cannot ever quite ig. nore inside this grave
-yard Park. but even now if you look closer. beyond this book

she's murmur
-ing. beyond the cane
-rows of the hair she's still up. braiding in the mirrow

she is canvassing beyond the language of the summer's clock
-work warm & curl she's bearing to the water
. you will already see the shadowes

even by the lakeside . even by the fountain
even by the footfall . even by the cart thats selling
snowball ice-cream sky-juice pindar coca~cola

even w/in the broadcast service of the cedar breeze
the black/white wayside tables plying chess
even w/in the holocaust of hot minetta bushes'

memories of streams
even within the deepest orange brocade russets
of her dream

.

each year upon this longest day . lover of leaf-light
golden beyond zodiac. emerald in pisces. indigo in platinegro
where he feels most strongest. most certain. most lion. most light-

ning. most royal. most ra. sheen. most àxé. most Xangô
when she's most loyal jasmine. most crest
and silvershed. most mellow full moon rising crowded

there will be this cloud . this sudden colour
down. fall cold & pouring . bright & fading .
each year upon this longest day . these lovers

NYC 21 June 1994 . 21 june 07 version . rev again 26 sept 08 . 21 june 09 . 15 march 2010

ARK

for Alice Coltrane & thanking Katy. Cecily and Annette Nias

And so this foreday daoud morning w/out light
or choice . i cannot swim
the stone. i can't hold on to water. so i drown

i swallow left. i turn & fall-
ow into fear & blight. a night so deep it make you turn
& weep the line of spiders of yr future you see spinn-

ing here. their silver
voice of tears. their lid. less jewel eyes .
all thru this buffeting eternity i toss i burn

again & when i rise leviathan from the deep . black shining from my skin
of seals. blask toothless pebbles mine the shore
haunted by dust & bromes . wrist. watches w/out tone

or tides. communion w/out broken hands. x-
plosions of frustration. the sufferation of the sweat
of hate. the absent ruby lips upon the wrinkle rim

of wine . i wake to tick to tell you that
in these loud waters of my land. there is no root no hope
no cloud no dream no sail canoe or miracle .

good day cannot repay bad *night*. our teeth snarl snapp-
ing even at halp. less angels' evenings' melting steel .
in this new farmer garden of the earths' delights

this staggering stranger of injustices come rumbelling down the wheel
& grave-
yard of the wind. down the scythe narrow streets

clear air for a moment . clear
innocence whe we are running. *so so so so so many*. the crowd flow-
ing over Brooklyn Bridge

so so so many . i had not thought death had undone so
many. melting away into what is now sighing . lights gone from the clear
avenue forever . our souls sometimes far out ahead of our white rat-

tle sur-
faces. and not looking back. looking back. looking back
as it is in Bhuj. in Grenada. Guernica. Amritsar

Tajitzkhan. the sulphur-stricken cities of the plains
of Aetna. Pelée. ab Napolis. the widow baby-
mothers of the slaves not lookin back in Bosnia. the Sudan. Chernobyl

Oaxaca terremoto. al'fata el Jenin. the Bhopal
babies sucking toxic milk . *our growing tongues*
accustom to the *what-is-the-word-that-is-not-here-in-English*

beyond shade and *schadenfreude* . not at all like *duende*
pleasure domes of massacre. acres & acres of its aching x-
actment. meaning the rusty-tasting smell of dead

blood . skull . the loneliness of broken hull. cracks. blue
wind through its stark ripe terror. simple blind doom
in the most secret houses of the brain . in the loud wild

thunder of the lung's now quasimodo faces of the moon
shape of the mosque. its pain. shape
of my mother's womb. strange

lingering words mean. ing havoc hymen hyenas & howling . altar
of human scream & scar-
ifice . 2000 fahrenheit of sheening fuel sun-

light . cenote . abattoir . golgotha
yr wife crying out in vein from the hammock of her home
out of her own vain loneliness of dream

that she have gone some whe far away
still writhing the screams of her chilldren
still listening for threads in the language of dis. placement & fissure

her face crack & squeeze like the dry mud
of abossom. the dread sodden puddles of camels
even tho the barnacle elephants still walk glistening glisten-

ing out of the water. her vice throttle to its very thorax
in this pillage. all this fine falling steel
the paper offices still soffly listening for midnight

still falling falling falling falling on tomorrow

O Leopold Sédar Senghor García Lorca Victor Hernández Cruz
still fall. ing fall. ing fall. ing . still soffly viequez .
Kurtz in his kongo clarinet of pain. the horrow

.

but what is the word
that you will nvr retrieve here ground zero. *shatila* .
more meaning of massacre auschwitz. shallow mass

graves. **babanghita.** the way you make me swallow
the tail of my tongue in the villages. following the foot-
steps of my self of my own river of flesh. my own ash my own alph my own

poem

and what is the word
for this high rafter of suicide. the rope
choking the throat of success. the shook

of yr death in the fission of indebtedness. quag-
mire . waste. quick-
sand. **My Brother**'s soft bowels of aids. the taste

of the death of uncouth in the copper of water
what prophet my tongue w/the tsunami loss
of my Mother the Noun. the flail-

ure of falling angelicas' hope. alphabets stuff upside-down
in my mouth. the babel of balasier & the down-
fall of plaster upon all these voices & scores. dub hip-

hop scouse. the markets of marrakesh settling old sores
of no longer verbs that can heal. of no longer baptisms
that will bawd out yr name from the cup of the flour of disaster. adjectives

already gone a-
way clattering. lounging in shame. the silence of rot
in the hot of unheavens. the dread kapot ovens of the beast

upon the thrashing floor of syphilis. thin
fur of fear upon the unknown animal that is now
yr very sister at the haven's door

four

little bombard girls of Birmingham that klu
klux christian tabernacle night in Sodom & Herero
the corn-

husk terror of Rwanda. the poor who live w/in
the stony guts & gashes of our or-
nate palaces. the pink hat widow now forever reach-

ing in frus. tration desperation on her open-window back-
seat for her hero husband's blown-out brains in Dallas
the curling Black Death mushroom gloom of God

in Nagasaki . what Pol Pot did . who Pol Pot died. King Leopold's
Great Pyramid of Skulls inside the Belgian Congo
like judas come to chrissmass. like leopard come to lamb

even upon this dark
un. even catastrophic ground
where soon the devastation saurus faces of the dead

will haunt us fron-
tom from their rat. tle sockets. the gentle liquird iris language
of their prayers . soft

blades of cyandles shimmering in psalms & pain & irie innocence
of ruin photographs & childhood teddy bears' young lighted flickering
eyes against the black & shining iron railings' incense in the parks

all their birds gone
leaves' spirits of green vegetation's ceremonies . gone
it look like nearly evva one who went to work up they dat day is gone

Rita Lasar Joseph O'Reilly Masuda wa Sultan. her 19 children gone
the Ladder 16 crew. *so many thousands gone* . and nothing nothing nothing
now in iraQ Darfur Manhattan in Afghanistan. . .

nyc september 2001

six

This sweet
windpersonpoem

for DreamChad and Mary Morgan Brathwaite

This sweet air comes from a long sweet time so ago so ago before scissors

before tractors & wheels before horses
are tamed & cattle are penned
in this ramshackle brown by the airport

it comes from sweet lands of aroma
crossing Atlantic w/spiders & egrets
& coconuts & thin tendril plants
on the slavetradewind of the harmattan

it comes from how the land is sweet here . result of all these long ancient
pressures of our coral times. lime
-stone & sweet-lime & loam
like a dark butter for green grasses of alloama

- how the sharp sweet cutlash scent
of the sugarcane comes down the reap shallow valleys
into our yards into the wide open arms of our houses

*T*his sweet air comes in w/the white birds of seaweed

& the blackbirds of tune
-less & the sudden wet clatter of parakeets
& the quick quick step & peck

-ing of sparrows
& these little blue chips that at dawn sing like rainbows
or water of a sweet thought down the long throttle throat of an egret

- how you remember this sound from Browns
Beach - the green bottle in yr hand yr head down
under. water &

sinking - all yr body heavy & drifting slowly glow
-ing down down down towards the bottom of the sand
& the bottle singing of lands-end w/in you in yr hand

& blinking w/the stars
& the sweet sound of the dawn
-bird filling it down

& the slow horses all the way from korlegonnu
& koromantin and gorée gorée gorée
coming up over the reefs of yr birth and opening their vision. singing

*T*his sweet wind comes to confirm all these memories of glass
how it is present at this corner by the shop and the gas
station . how it comes out from the hills

the long rising lines of ancient beaches into terraces
& the landscape of the future growing up towards us from Harrismith
from Congo Bay from Chancery Lane

where Margaret Gill sees all this as she sits sewing words
& Indrani her Malayalam neighbour
sets up her palette of paints for her NCF mural at RockDundo

as dreams from the sea drift up over the old sea-egg Silver Sands coast
rounding South Point & the white waves
of Oistins . the breakers coming in from blue distance

onto the bright powder silica beaches where the dunes
are. their power curling their sound into silence. their mists drifting inward
into our mangrove & seagrape

& the blue spotted cactus & noo-noo
& the unpainted wooden houses we have built along this shoar
to catch this silence sound to breathe this sweet air

smile w/ it. shoring it up. as it were . grow. ing greater w/ it into the green
& blue where the sunlight unlocks.   where the flowers are
& the bees playing all this attention to their fix(ed) favourite colours

& the slow certain dance of the ants
who prefer their long black slightly trembling line
of silhouette & that fine instant fizz of them this morning

when they are not
dead or disturbed. devouring what has been left from the fall
of a fruit or the lipstick of blossom or the splash of some passion

and when i look up again the world is like a tuning fork
the itself of its memory receding ceeding ceeding ceeding
into its own sound its so certain & purpose & real

𝒯his sweet wind of sunlight which is here so long before we are born

so long even before we ever come here. before we loss
the names of the lannscape
on this Sunday morning of silence & worship

when we can still hear the old dour churchbells high up
in the toss of their steepleless ringing
at their certain times certain times certain times of angelicus

Watch how the birds fly up high & wheel

away from the bronze iron sound even tho they have heard it before
everyday & for centuries

like in S Marco in the steep solitudes of the Andes
and LLasha . the deep tones as if coming out
of the llama of wells . like the opposite of being drowned. fall

-in up. ward.   full of tree & sweet air . the free so amaze
-ingly green in yr ears.   their tangles their crystal clear branches
these churchyards sleeping in the sun where the wooden

stalls of their helmet-shape bells
- cast in brass cast in bronze cast in iron
- are like at St Leonards like at St Clements in St Lucy

like at St Margarets overlooking Martins Bay w/the rope & the little gate
& the triangle top nvr yet they say blown down in a hurricane
my half-blind cousin Daddy O'Grady Elizabelle O'Neale

muse & musician violinist organist & organizer at All Saints
w/the sweetest voice in the world in her throat
dark woo-dove of contraltocello coming down the hill

from the Maynards curve & the corner down Ben Hill
all the way down from the church
it is twenty minutes she take in the hot sun after the service

is over but she comes floatin down singing aloud to her
-self and her saviour
w/her ivory

chaplet & hymn
-book in that so scapular silence of Sunday
& the shak-shak in shadows of gold . waiting for her at the door

of her father's unpainted carpenter shop. close(d) now from the birds
because it is Sunday . so she goes round to the back
up that slow rocky rickety path. way between our two houses & forever homes

that the Government now intends to make into a new road & high
-way to link M&Q w/the new housing estates of Fair
-field & Indian Ground & Mt Brevitor

where all that time now agro almost pass(ed)
me & my sister like Wordsworth & his
Mary Maria Dor

-othea. dis
-covering this path up the hill where only the silk grasses gorows
. the soft sound of 'esses'

and reaching the top. see our New
-stead & the red roof-tops of the Vicarage. and beyond that & its trees
the differently sweet sweet wind from the sea

mixed w/the scent
of the grass and that sea
distant & blue & flattering . an we running already into the pic

-ture
the future.   whe we are heading already thru the fat
valley of canes in the hollow below us .   towards the everlastingly high

-lands of the Brevitor hills
w/their scarred white sacred limestone faces
whe they tell you in the village *there's a place name BrevitorCave out there*

but no. body willin to show us or don't have no time fe the roam
so we find it ourselves one hot morning w/Fillmore
running upthe path along the lookin-down cliff

-face & lookin lookin lookin up
until high
up where there is no

more path. the dark open face of the adit we climb up. as if we was climb
-ing down water as many years later
i climb up again w/ Dream

Chad but by then it was lost
we were out
of that frame & wd nvr find that secret again

as we had when we was young in those green
glorious tracks down the hill w/ my sister
her eyes dark & wide & clear & sweatin soffly under her round pan

-amma hat w/the elastic under her chin
which my dear-aunts say she had was to wear
when she *ruinnin bout here in de broilin hot*

-sun . an i think they say i had was to wear my black felt cap too
- *nor yr bare-back shiney ball-headed plate out in god heaven yu hear muh!*
an we fine the cave & its huge self . w/the bats huggin high in the dark

cries of the shelfs
& the wenn ceiling & the cracks of light comin thru from the height like some un
-hewn & wonderful cathedral . the festoons of candelabra

& the green like cobwebs of algebra eyes
in the hang
-ing limestone cataracts. & the damp

echo or sometimes no echo at all in our voices of juvenile barter
- w/something here much much bigger than we had ever known
before in our corner . beyond even ball

-room or church or St Michael cathedral . that kind of interior size
- as if we wasn't any longer in our island at all or down in Mile & Quarter
from school & on holidays. as if we was somethings or some. bodies else

all together. the poem turning into a dreamstorie of forever
even as i write it this way. w/so little regular hundred-metres or rhyme(s)
but w/sort-of margims & lines

so that its
undergrounn riddim can capture some of what hides
here in the dark as it happens at once

thru so many different & at the same time time
-tumbling & simultaneous space
-palaces - the world of whirl & interface of memories

we call 'writing a poem'
. and when we come back out of the cave
this will remain wlus all our Brevitor lives

where all our friends are & our loved ones & our parents
- back there wlall of us in that strange special place of our island
already losing sight of it

-self wlthis building of houses this building building of houses
& the white access angelus roads of our death
. so that already. as i say. me & DreamChad cdn't find it

that NewYears Day morning before we get marrèd
high up above Time at the Old Windmill
on that OrangeHill ridge. maybe even higher than Brevitor

•

- and tho none a dem come w/us on these journeys
into up here. they was always here w/us
whenever we step down an inta that cave of creator

into that strange dark of dahomey. the cool the a-glow
- they was always there. always here. as i say w/our few-
ture

&

So we step back out into this land . scape air so sweep so sweep

this Sunday morning of brown . from its long sweet time so ago so ago
before scissors before tractors & hand-
cyarts before horses are tamed & cattle are penned

so long before me writing this poem in this ramshackle pass-
ture of wind thru the grass
by this Pilgrim Place airport of ishak meshak & abednegro

Seven

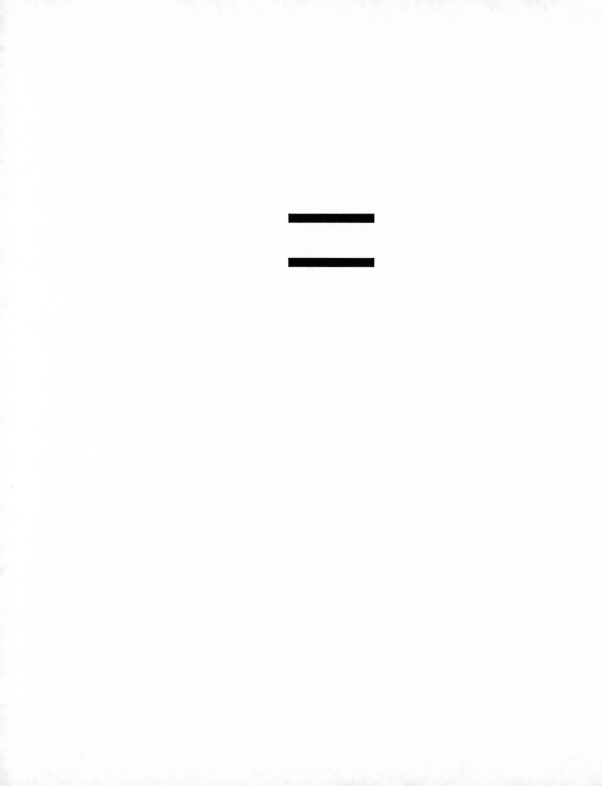

Tell me how close (1)

my life here now
in the shade i can tell my sad
widow wife of the morning. is now

like a thin sheet of white
paper - *why 'white' i don't know* - tumbling transparent & dumb as the day
glows reed. or like a long

shadow of glass lying on the ground of a window
-pane. or the slight sheet of a frozen river on which the beats
of my heart like the blank

fleet of hannibal's lame elephants walk on that slow retreat of the horse
-men from moscow over the alphs over the hoarse mestizo sierra across
the grey tundril steppes

of mangolia. wait/ing to punch me thru to kalunga
waiting to plunge me thru to the thick slugging streams
of kurtz horrow

and all that i have left tomorrow
will be the lurch
-ing efforts i have made to keep these elephants

from happening brimstone. each foot. step a dark patch on the crack
-ing chart of my history . on the pin & pen & pain of my memory
the inQuisitorial brain of how i stretch out and rustle all day and all night

on the tumb
-rill river of dreams to prevent this tendril moment of mabrak
this dark and this light

Tell me how close (2)/a po for DreamChad since Mark gone

it is as if you dead and i hear yr voice at the door of the next
room. up from the street. along the path of the stone
Park. loitering on the Mona stream in a small boat. in a canoe

. lying in a scarce crop-over harvest punt
up in a tree w/birds
hello hello hello . the curve going upwards soft & faint

-ly twittering soft & tremulo diminuendo
. but it's yr sun that's gone - the suddem savage blow
the pain the groin gouged out yr womb

so suddenly w/out sound and like a bomb
-down echoes that goes on forever down the well
that now will have no nvr end

will have no sound of bell but calls of *why why why*
& where is me & why is me & *why why why*
am i not here to stop it save him hold him free him from this last

fierce harm. this neck i hold from birth
from softest painful breaking thirst
so broeken here w/out a cry and always cry

-ing now in this dark midnight street
Hope Garden Garden Gate
for. ever hurting haunting mwe down these long Papine Market

alleyways . where
i can no longer ear
im song when i shd ave im ere

to love im back to blindness & to me. back to the in
-stann he is born to start again upon a diffrent road
that will not bare this mad. ness on my breast

this metal-breathing & toyota beast
come scar
-face snarl. ing up from Liguanea to brek im back im neck my heart

my torn
apart. a radio like a open mouth that calls *Hello*
but cannot hear you like before i happy

comin off the burn
-ing street from shoppin or comin thru the door from church
before i tek my hat off lookin in yr room from visiting my brother

an comin in to you . why do you lurch so till
in. side this shatta dark whe you are shadow
-less & scorm. why don't you answer this red staring cry

O pour some oshun honey on this cross
-roads whe i am straggellin
. why can't you hear my thorn

Tell me how close (3)

The tastes of yr flesh is fish
now in my mouth and i re-
turn away from you as towards the loose

of my mother's milk. my sperm
settle back down in my belly . stale
now & diverse . O how i wish

i had nvr abuse
you. use you like river cherries
in my mouth from so long

ago so ago and will nvr now grow
from that moment when yr breasts
were so ready & cêlêbês to mother my chilldren

round & large & luminous on the cool
sheets you had so specially smooth(ed)
out & prepared w/scents from the medelline. the nipples

as i had nvr seen them before. not even on the grass
in the moon-
light. as if in the menstrual months of my absence

you had spooned them w/this soft sensual flow
of pommegranate -
this loveliest grenade beyond the *lwa* & the law

and had surrendered all yr agony
then.   all yr soft swimming bones to this one sweet
cruel crisis that wd have born us terrible twins

leaving our mothers in wonder. hiding their pride
& their secrets of pleasure but dividing the island
drawing daggers all along the seashores the horizons glint-

ing w/their language of gossip & the thunderous gossamer rumours
of in-
coming storms

How all this wd have been one kind of world. perhaps - no - certainly -
kindlier - you wd have been bourne happy into yr entitlement of silver hairs
and there wd have been no threat

or flaw of cancer or forgetfulness or dementia or enemy break-in
no danger then of that sort and i wd have published our love-
songs in their paradox no matter whe they take us .

the x/hiliration - the fortunate accident of so many new & trans-
patient metaphors . not the thin little run-down garden cling-
ing against the hot grey walls of yr lonely afternoon home

but a whole new pasture of egrets & seahawks & parrakeets & almond
trees with their oriental eyes the paradaisal smell of ole-
ander lebanon & alexandria all over the limitless green .

But i failed you on those frozen sheets
i cdn't get it up i cdnt get it in .
until you had to turn away with the tears of our twins in yr eyes

and the future fall. ing like the stars of the last days
until you was at last or again this likkle old woman
sitting in the corner with the toothless broom & the scars

and all the critics ganging up to happ-
ily put down my books or worse sideline & ignore
me and you nvr speaking to me anymore from yr womb until this morning

when at last you come to visit in the guise of a new tv cyar in the driveway
a new woman . a young girl an interior decorator of scores
dressed in the white of spiritual survival with sleight sandals of gold-

en up the steps of my adobe up into the crunching marl of my loneliness
and i reach out again to touch to embrace & embellish your kiss
this taste of fish of trieste that you have become

this punishment of promise & renewal
that you now bringing me too late in my life for bonfires
or birthday parties of virtue too late in my life for fireworks & celebration &

hot panties . too vertigo
for cocktails xcept the white cock himself murdered like me by mad
dogs on the pasture before we cd wake to the rescue

and the sun coming up now on the saddest day of the year in wrinkles
& un. recovery life-sentences between the leaves
of the sandbox & the cassia trees & the droning of doves of archbishops of flies

eight

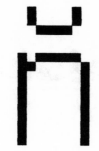

fflute(s)

pam mordecai

is when the bamboo from its clip of yellow groan and wrestle
begins to glow
and the wind learns the shape of its fire

and my fingers following the termites drill
find their hollows
of silence. shatters of echoes of tone   .

that my eyes close
all along the wall . all along the branches . all along the world
and that that creak of spirits walking these graves of sunlight

spiders over the water. cobwebs crawling in whispers
over the stampen green . find
from a distance so cool it is a hill in haze

it is a fish of shadow along the sandy bottom
that the wind is following my footsteps
all along the rustle all along the echoes all along the world

and that that stutter i had heard in some dark summer freedom
startles and slips from fingertip to finger-
stop. into the float of the morning into the throat of its sound

< >

it is a baby mouth but softer than the suck
it makes

it is a hammock sleeping in the woodland
it is a hammer shining in the shade
it is the kite ascending chord and croon

and screamer(s)

it is the cloud that curls to hide the eagle
it is the ripple of the stream from bamboo
it is the ripple of the stream from blue

it is the gurgle pigeon dream the ground dove coo
it is the sun approaching midday listening its splendour
it is your voice alight with echo

w/the birth of sound

JJ 1986

nine

The writing of the sea shd not result

in its escarpment
she said

mmveene allu tuka xtbox . alongongono

The scene of water fine & blue behind her
standing before me unxpected on the beach
her three eyes glowing

like Hyppolite her step
-father of the earth
the painther of heaven & hellven

thussaluttata

i know i can't pass a foot any longer beyond her
her hair was as green as they always said
and it sparkle w/pink coral & the morning time

- but can't i -

TranssaluttatA

the same sword again
in its stronger drift & different meaning
of foam upon the water

and i cd hear the lonely drone of the breakers in her flesh
and she was dark brown and naked
all down to the navel of her course

You nuse two head to swim
Why select only one now for the gender?

It was as if i understanding her to say *anthology*

weer attalatata . *guernei* . that >rest< there . *guernei*
on the future of impossibility

The dancer muss stop this foolish & dance

What has this got to do w/verdant w/water?
i can't dance the nation

!wa.(Ƹ)aXian!

Nvr before had the tide run so smoothly
all the colours w/out fish
the high blue head of the rain
-bow pulling off the top of the sky

!wa.(Ƹ)aXian!

It wasn't suppose to be like this
She shd have been repeating like the women i know
not w/these pink. red. fierce indigo eyes
strange hint black butterflies

the sea w/out bees or divination
the white sharp teeth
the wrenck smell of the Passage shark
where was my **HELP** on this short

stretch of pale beach. w/the sea
-almond(s) almost down to the water's edge
the cold at her feet
clear & sweet ijala round the safety of her anchours

!aja 𝕏lla!

She was so close to me now
. tho she hadn't move any feather or farther .
i cd hear in the belle all the distance she have travail

¿mwallalla¿

Only walkin

¿feelar¿

i smile(d)

She already know about the poem i wd nvr be writing
the signs & signatures i cd nvr recapture
all the plants groaning in the loam of the limestone
i wd nvr rain

mercie!

i crie soffly
a veil of water w/out flame

lwa
she say simply
anba dlo

obinrinbinrin ni yòò ∂á e jò yú

i nodded w/out name
transfix & blessèd before the Belovèd
. becoming together

a ?sSimple ooman will judge dis-ya case
1 Spr 2010

ten

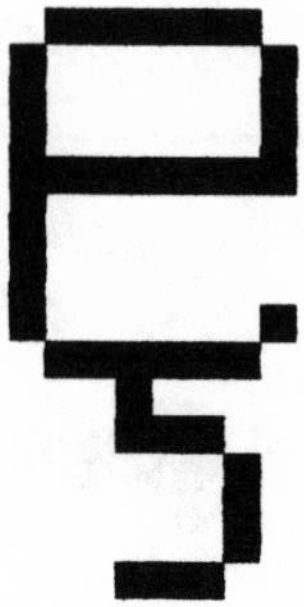

Letter to Zea Mexican

(3)

LHE CROSSING

One late afternoon i drive Aunt May &
DreamChad up to Hardwar Gap & the
Park up there Looking across from whe-
re we were there was a soft valley of acc-
ord & beyond that on the same level w/
us a wood in mist & you cd see a road &
the light under the trees in the distance
but it was like over there & you cdnt see
the connection how it get where it was <
how you cd get there & there was no on
(e) over there Only peace As if **there** <<
was where she was walking away from
us but perhaps waiting but each day get
ing more & more distance & getting more
& more involve w/what was happening
over there & meeting the people out ther
(e) over there & gettin to know them &
her Mother eventually getting the news
that she had arrive & setting out to find <

her in that landscape over there so near
so far far away in the grey green going-
>down evening sun forever & for ever<
Heartease Which is where she is/in that
soft distance shining & i'm suddenly & at
last happy & very very sad & lonely at th
(e) same time because she feelin so lonely
but somehow at peace & there was noth
ing i cd do nothing nothing i cd do any <
more nothing i cd ever do ever & ever a-
gain but to lose her there & that way wh-
ere i cd see her & not see her beyond th-
at valley high up here in the
Blue
Mountains

from ZMO – the final sequence . entitle NYC June 03 . 07

123

ALSO BY KAMAU BRATHWAITE
Poetry

Rights of Passage
Masks
Islands
The Arrivants
The Arrivants/Die Ankömmlinge
Penguin Modern Poets 15
Days & Nights
Other Exiles
Black + Blues
Mother Poem
Soweto
Word Making Man: Poem for Nicolás Guillén in Xaymaca
Sun Poem
Third World Poems
Jah Music
Korabra
Le détonateur de visibilité/The Visibility Trigger
X/Self
Sappho Sakyi's Meditations
Shar/Hurricane Poem
Middle Passages
Primisi-ô: Sranantongo translation of Rights of Passage
Words need love too
Ancestors
Ark
Born to Slow Horses
Los Danzantes del Tiempo: a Spanish/English Selection

KAMAU BRATHWAITE, born in Barbados in 1930, is an internationally celebrated poet, performer, and cultural theorist. Co-founder of the Caribbean Artists Movement, he was educated at Pembroke College, Cambridge, and has a PhD from the University of Sussex in the U.K. He has served on the board of directors of UNESCO's History of Mankind project since 1979, and as a cultural advisor to the government of Barbados from 1975 to 1979 and since 1990.

His awards include the Griffin Prize, the Neustadt International Prize for Literature, the Bussa Award, the Casa de las Americas Prize, and the Charity Randall Prize for Performance and Written Poetry. He has received both Guggenheim and Fulbright fellowships, among many others. His book The Zea Mexican Diary (1993) was the Village Voice Book of the Year. Over the years, he has worked in the Ministry of Education in Ghana and taught at the University of the West Indies, Southern Illinois University, University of Nairobi, Holy Cross College, Yale University, and was a visiting W.E.B. Du Bois fellow at Harvard University. Brathwaite is currently Professor of Comparative Literature at New York University, and shares his time between his home in CowPastor, Barbados, and New York City.

ABOUT THE DRIFTLESS SERIES

The Driftless Series is a publication award program established
in 2010 and consists of five categories:

DRIFTLESS NATIONAL, for a second poetry book by a United States citizen
DRIFTLESS NEW ENGLAND, for a poetry book by a New England author
DRIFTLESS ENGLISH, for English language poetry from an author outside
the United States
DRIFTLESS TRANSLATION, for a translation of poetry into English
DRIFTLESS CONNECTICUT, for an outstanding book in any field by a
Connecticut author

The Driftless Series is funded by the Beatrice Fox Auerbach Foundation Fund
at the Hartford Foundation for Public Giving. For more information and a complete
list of books in The Driftless Series, please visit us online at
http://www.wesleyan.edu/wespress/driftless.